BRITAIN'S RELATIVE ECONOMIC DECLINE
1870-1995:
A QUANTITATIVE PERSPECTIVE

by Nicholas Crafts

©The Social Market Foundation

First published in March 1997
by
The Social Market Foundation
20, Queen Anne's Gate
London SW1H 9AA
Tel: 0171-222 7060 Fax: 0171-222 0310

Paper No. 29

ISBN 1 874097 76 3

Cover design by Adrian Taylor

Printed in Great Britain by
Xenogamy plc
Suite 2, Westcombe House
7-9 Stafford Road, Wallington, Surrey SM6 9AN
Typesetting by Wimyk Enterprises

CONTENTS

THE AUTHOR

NICHOLAS CRAFTS is Professor of Economic History at the London School of Economics. His books include *British Economic Growth during the Industrial Revolution* and *Can De-Industrialisation Seriously Damage Your Wealth?* Educated at Trinity College, Cambridge, he is a Fellow of the British Academy.

ACKNOWLEDGEMENTS

I am grateful to Robert Skidelsky for helpful comments on an earlier draft. Any errors are my sole responsibility.

Foreword

How to arrest and reverse Britain's relative economic decline has occupied the minds of policy-makers and politicians ever since it was first diagnosed towards the end of the last century.

To improve its economic performance the UK has sought at various times either to emulate aspects of competitors' policies or to outdo them by playing to what are regarded as Britain's natural strengths. Establishing the appropriate policy mix between imitation and innovation lies at the heart of the current debate about the best economic future for Britain. Whom should we be copying and how far should we go?

It is against this background that Professor Nicholas Crafts has written a paper which attempts to provide a sound quantitative analysis of Britain's economic performance over the past 120 years. In doing so he looks for clues as to how much of the nation's economic decline was inevitable — and, by implication, irreversible — and how much can be put down to policy errors and institutional weaknesses.

Surveying the last 20 years, Crafts says that UK growth rates are matching those of our major European competitors for the first time since the War, but that Britain is still being outstripped by the Asian Tigers with their rapid growth of physical and human capital.

In all, says Crafts, the UK is enjoying sufficient growth in productivity and the quality of investment to have halted her decline relative to Europe. Whether the country's growth rate can be raised further is a more open and difficult question.

Roderick Nye
February 1997

Introduction

The aim of this paper is, in essence, quite simple, namely to provide a fair and objective description of long-run economic performance in Britain. An exercise of this kind is not, however, as straightforward as might appear at first sight. This introduction is intended to alert readers to some of the issues that arise and decisions that have to be made in carrying out the task. These involve the conceptualisation of the approach, the choice of indicators to present and the need to put raw data into an appropriate context.

General interest in comparisons of economic performance both over time and across countries has probably never been greater. Recent years have seen a proliferation of reports on 'competitiveness' and in Britain the topic has been given added spice by the rhetoric of Conservative governments since 1979 which have seen themselves as reversing a long period of relative economic decline. Indeed, since 1994 the British government has produced an annual Competitiveness White Paper which has tried to maintain a precarious balance between claiming that things are much better than they once were but that much more needs to be done to catch up with other countries. Its presentation of the UK's track record is, of course, a political rather than an academic document.

The definition of 'national competitiveness' which the British government uses follows the OECD and is the following:

> the degree to which the country can, under free and fair market conditions, produce goods and services which meet the test of international markets, while simultaneously maintaining and expanding the real incomes of its people over the long term.

The original Competitiveness White Paper goes on to point out that to be competitive in this sense requires continuing long-term productivity improvement and a performance that compares favourably with that of other countries (DTI, 1994, p. 9).

This definition has been subject to vigorous criticism by economists, most notably by Krugman (1994). Improvement in living standards would generally be regarded as a central objective of economic policy and, appropriately defined, as the chief criterion by which economies should be judged. It is also valuable to recognise that a sustained rise in the long-run growth rate of real incomes matters much more for economic welfare than do short-term but transitory changes in output.

There is no good reason, however, to single out performance in external trade, which is a subset of overall activity, as having special importance and undue emphasis on the balance of external payments or world market share may encourage protectionist tendencies which are harmful to growth and welfare in the long run. On occasions, trends in external trade and payments may be an important diagnostic indicating that the growth rate is unsustainable or perhaps reflecting weaknesses in innovation or investment. But at most, external trade performance is a warning signal and/or a constraint; it is not an ultimate objective of policy nor is it, *per se*, a measure of economic welfare.

Traditionally, economists have taken the long-run or trend rate of growth of real gross domestic product (GDP) per person to be the best available measure of an economy's achievement in raising living standards and the level of real GDP per person to be the appropriate comparator of economic performance across countries at a point in time. Making estimates of these outcomes obviously entails important technical issues, the most important of which are briefly discussed in Chapter One.

At the same time, economists have also recognised that there are strong reasons to consider augmenting the national accounts concept of real GDP to obtain a more comprehensive measure of changes in real incomes or economic welfare. Two contributions to this literature are particularly worth noting.

Nordhaus and Tobin (1972) emphasised that, in principle, it is important to recognise that an economy with the same GDP but more leisure per person would generally be regarded as having higher economic welfare and to remember that both over time and also across countries leisure time has varied a great deal.

Modern work on economic development following Sen (1987) and Dasgupta (1993) stresses the importance in the quality of life of capabilities rather than incomes *per se* and notes that the correlation between income growth and enhancement of capabilities may sometimes be weak. In particular, outcomes in terms of education and health which might be taken to be fundamental to the quality of life may depend much more on the provision of public services than on the command of private incomes.

Taking some account of these arguments is certainly possible in practice and is attempted in Chapter One. It must be accepted, however, that there is no general consensus on how best to proceed and that measurement (index number) problems loom larger than with the (less ambitious) traditional approach based simply on GDP.

Although the stress of the 'national competitiveness' approach on economic growth focuses on an aspect of economic performance that is central to enhancing living standards, other outcomes may also matter a good deal. Indeed, ultimately, value judgements are required to weight these relative to economic growth.

It might be argued that most people are risk-averse and would give up some extra growth for a reduction of economic insecurity if such a choice were available. Moreover, if less inequality in the distribution of incomes is regarded as a good thing, an acceleration of trend growth where the rich gain more than the poor may be seen as a deterioration by those who value equality highly.

In considering recent changes in economic performance, evidence on outcomes other than productivity growth will therefore be presented so that those who wish to weigh one against another can do so.

The notion of British relative economic decline is inherently one based on international comparisons. Whether the criterion is real GDP per person or some broader measure of economic welfare there is no doubt that, in common with all the OECD countries, absolute living standards have improved over time. The disappointment for Britain has been that growth elsewhere has been faster and that as a result Britain has tended over time to slide down the league tables relating to levels of attainment. Nowhere was this more true than during the 'Golden Age' of European economic growth in the years after World War II when British economic growth was higher than ever before and yet the acceleration in growth elsewhere was much stronger.

A key reason to be interested in comparisons, whether over time or across countries, is that a yardstick can be obtained against which to assess what may have been possible and thus to evaluate performance. This 'benchmarking' aspect is indeed implicit in the DTI's view of 'competitiveness'. To be meaningful, however, it is vital to choose an appropriate peer group or to allow for differences in circumstances. Thus, in comparing growth rates, it might be held that the economic environment in the 'Golden Age' was much more benign than that before or since. It might also be argued that economically immature countries which exploit opportunities for catching-up (such as Japan in the early post-war period) can grow at rates which are not feasible for the already advanced economies.

It should already be clear that useful comparisons of economic performance involve theorising in order to allow raw data to inform on 'success' or 'failure'. This is even more the case when questions relating to sustainability are concerned. Thus it would be important, for example, at a minimum, to consider trends in the proximate determinants of long-term growth as well as recent growth outcomes in any attempt to establish whether relative economic decline in Britain has been reversed since 1979.

It is also apparent that any appraisal of the Conservative governments' record in attempting to change the long-run rate of growth is fraught with difficulty. We have already seen that it is necessary to take a view on the following issues:

♦ Is it better to look at the conventional measure of real GDP per person or to augment this by further considerations?

♦ What are the appropriate yardsticks against which to compare and assess British growth post-1979?

♦ Are there reasons to believe that any improvement in growth is likely to be sustained?

♦ Are any changes in growth worthwhile or have they cost too much in terms of adverse changes in other outcomes?

Three further points also need to be borne in mind. First, although there are reasons to believe that governments can influence growth at least somewhat, it may be very difficult to change the growth rate by very much and many policy changes may only pay off in the very long run (Crafts, 1996b). Second, it must be recognised that all governments face political constraints on what policies can be adopted, but that allowing for these is essentially a matter of subjective opinion rather than a case of testable hypotheses. Finally, the political debate is essentially not about actual performance but revolves around counterfactuals — would the outcomes have looked better under a hypothetical different government?

Chapter One: Relative Economic Decline: An Initial Overview

This chapter provides a basic statistical outline of comparative economic performance since 1870. The presentation of material reflects choices made with regard to the issues discussed in the introduction on which there is some further elaboration along the way. Most of the estimates are taken from well-known authoritative sources. Obviously, there are imperfections in all historical statistics and, in general, these are more serious the further back one goes. The basic data in Tables 1 to 3 do represent the best that is currently on offer, although they may yet be further revised as new information becomes available.

Table 1 gives a series of snapshots of relative levels of real GDP per person in benchmark years from 1870 to 1994. The estimates are based on historical national accounts data. The countries selected for comparison are determined partly by data availability and partly by including the OECD countries and recent Asian success stories with which Britain is regularly compared in everyday discussion. How far this is an appropriate peer group will be explored later on. Former communist countries are excluded because of data problems, although the source from which these numbers have been taken does include provisional estimates. The table is not a complete listing of all those with high income levels in each year; for example, in 1913 Argentina's real GDP per person was $3797 and in 1950 Venezuela's was $7424 (Maddison, 1995, pp. 202-3).

The unit of measurement in Table 1 is 'International Dollars of 1990'. This means that current price estimates in own currencies of GDP in different countries in 1990 have been converted into dollars using a measure of the purchasing power of the currency rather than the prevailing nominal exchange rate. As the jargon has it, the

1990 estimates are 'purchasing power parity adjusted'. This is now standard practice in making international comparisons as it is well-known that the use of nominal exchange rates produces serious distortions and systematic biases. It must be remembered, however, that comparisons of purchasing power involve comparing the costs of baskets of goods and are subject to all the usual 'index number problems' to do with choices of weights, comparisons of quality etc. which imply that, in practice, there can sometimes be a range of estimates from which to choose.

Having obtained a measure of relative GDP per person for this base year, this is projected backwards to 1870 and forwards to 1994 using domestic estimates for the growth of real GDP in each country. Here too there are familiar index number problems in devising the appropriate price indices with which to deflate current price estimates of nominal GDP. Three particularly difficult issues concern the treatment of new goods, the measurement of quality changes over time and the assessment of real output in non-marketed services. The procedures adopted are not the same in all countries. Although the precise detail of the comparisons is sensitive to all these index number problems, the broad outline of relative performance shown in Table 1 is probably reasonably reliable for our purposes.

In assembling the estimates from which Table 1 is taken, Maddison (1995) attempted to construct figures for the current borders of these countries. Clearly, Germany is the most problematic case in this context. The estimates for Germany in Table 1 relate to the area of Western Germany prior to unification. Similarly, for the UK the estimates seek to exclude Southern Ireland prior to 1921.

Table 1 reflects a steady decline in real GDP per person in the UK relative to other countries against a background of large increases in absolute levels as economic growth has taken place. Thus real GDP per person in 1994 in the UK was five times the 1870 level yet the UK had slipped from 2nd in 1870 to 17th by 1994. Prior to 1950, the

Table 1. Levels of Real GDP/Person: Benchmark Years, 1870 1994

1870		1913		1950		1973		1994	
1. Australia	3801	1. Australia	5505	1. USA	9573	1. Switzerland	17953	1. USA	22569
2. UK	3263	2. USA	5307	2. Switzerland	8939	2. USA	16607	2. Switzerland	20830
3. New Zealand	3115	3. New Zealand	5115	3. New Zealand	8495	3. Canada	13644	3. Hong Kong	19592
4. Belgium	2640	4. UK	5032	4. Canada	7218	4. Sweden	13494	4. Japan	19505
5. Netherlands	2640	5. Canada	4213	5. Australia	7047	5. Denmark	13416	5. Denmark	19305
6. USA	2457	6. Switzerland	4207	6. UK	6847	6. Germany	13152	6. Germany	19097
7. Switzerland	2172	7. Belgium	4130	7. Denmark	6738	7. France	12940	7. Singapore	18797
8. Denmark	1927	8. Netherlands	3950	8. Sweden	6683	8. Australia	12763	8. Norway	18372
9. Germany	1913	9. Germany	3833	9. Netherlands	5850	9. Netherlands	12575	9. Canada	18350
10. Austria	1875	10. Denmark	3764	10. Belgium	5346	10. New Zealand	12485	10. France	17968
11. France	1858	11. Austria	3488	11. France	5221	11. Austria	11992	11. Austria	17285
12. Ireland	1775	12. France	3452	12. Norway	4969	12. Belgium	11905	12. Belgium	17225
13. Sweden	1664	13. Sweden	3096	13. Germany	4281	13. UK	11308	13. Netherlands	17152
14. Canada	1620	14. Ireland	2733	14. Finland	4131	14. Japan	11017	14. Australia	17107
15. Italy	1467	15. Italy	2507	15. Austria	3731	15. Finland	10768	15. Sweden	16704
16. Spain	1376	16. Norway	2275	16. Ireland	3518	16. Italy	10409	16. Italy	16404
17. Norway	1303	17. Spain	2255	17. Italy	3425	17. Norway	10229	17. UK	16371
18. Finland	1107	18. Finland	2050	18. Spain	2397	18. Spain	8739	18. New Zealand	15085
19. Portugal	1085	19. Greece	1621	19. Portugal	2132	19. Greece	7779	19. Finland	14779
20. Japan	741	20. Portugal	1354	20. Singapore	2038	20. Portugal	7568	20. Taiwan	12985
		21. Japan	1334	21. Hong Kong	1962	21. Ireland	7023	21. Ireland	12624
		22. South Korea	948	22. Greece	1951	22. Hong Kong	6768	22. Spain	12544
		23. Taiwan	794	23. Japan	1873	23. Singapore	5412	23. South Korea	11235
				24. Taiwan	922	24. Taiwan	3669	24. Portugal	11083
				25. South Korea	876	25. South Korea	2840	25. Greece	10165

Sources: derived from Maddison (1995) supplemented for Hong Kong, Singapore in 1973 by World Bank (1995) and for Hong Kong, Singapore, South Korea and Taiwan in 1994 by Asian Development Bank (1995).

Table 2. Human Development Index, 1870-1992

	1870	HDI		1913	HDI		1950	HDI		1970	HDI		1992	HDI
1.	Australia	0.530	1.	Australia	0.787	1.	Netherlands	0.855	1.	Canada	0.887	1.	Canada	0.932
2.	UK	0.493	2.	New Zealand	0.786	2.	New Zealand	0.854	2.	Sweden	0.881	2.	Switzerland	0.931
3.	USA	0.453	3.	USA	0.730	3.	Canada	0.851	3.	USA	0.881	3.	Japan	0.929
4.	Switzerland	0.447	4.	UK	0.717	4.	USA	0.851	4.	Denmark	0.879	4.	Norway	0.928
5.	Netherlands	0.445	5.	Switzerland	0.685	5.	UK	0.850	5.	Norway	0.878	5.	Sweden	0.928
6.	Denmark	0.444	6.	Denmark	0.683	6.	Sweden	0.847	6.	Japan	0.875	6.	France	0.927
7.	Belgium	0.417	7.	Netherlands	0.677	7.	Denmark	0.845	7.	France	0.873	7.	Australia	0.926
8.	Sweden	0.412	8.	Canada	0.672	8.	Norway	0.844	8.	Australia	0.872	8.	USA	0.925
9.	Canada	0.403	9.	Germany	0.637	9.	Australia	0.842	9.	Switzerland	0.871	9.	Netherlands	0.923
10.	Germany	0.390	10.	Sweden	0.634	10.	Switzerland	0.842	10.	UK	0.867	10.	UK	0.919
11.	France	0.387	11.	Belgium	0.618	11.	Belgium	0.827	11.	Netherlands	0.862	11.	Germany	0.918
12.	Norway	0.352	12.	France	0.611	12.	France	0.825	12.	New Zealand	0.861	12.	Austria	0.917
13.	Austria	0.248	13.	Norway	0.576	13.	Germany	0.772	13.	Austria	0.857	13.	Belgium	0.916
14.	Italy	0.179	14.	Ireland	0.553	14.	Austria	0.729	14.	Germany	0.856	14.	Denmark	0.912
15.	Japan	0.151	15.	Austria	0.493	15.	Finland	0.729	15.	Finland	0.855	15.	Finland	0.911
16.	Finland	0.149	16.	Italy	0.435	16.	Ireland	0.726	16.	Belgium	0.851	16.	New Zealand	0.907
			17.	Spain	0.381	17.	Italy	0.672	17.	Italy	0.831	17.	Ireland	0.892
			18.	Japan	0.372	18.	Japan	0.595	18.	Ireland	0.829	18.	Italy	0.891
			19.	Finland	0.353	19.	Spain	0.574	19.	Spain	0.820	19.	Spain	0.888
						20.	Greece	0.540	20.	Hong Kong	0.737	20.	Hong Kong	0.875
						21.	Hong Kong	0.471	21.	Greece	0.723	21.	Greece	0.874
						22.	Portugal	0.462	22.	Singapore	0.684	22.	Taiwan	0.872
						23.	Singapore	0.451	23.	Taiwan	0.622	23.	South Korea	0.859
						24.	South Korea	0.349	24.	Portugal	0.588	24.	Singapore	0.848
						25.	Taiwan	0.348	25.	South Korea	0.523	25.	Portugal	0.838

Source: Crafts (1996a) for 1870, 1913 and 1950; United Nations (1994) for 1970, 1992.

UK was only overtaken with the exception of Switzerland, by non-European countries. Between 1950 and 1979 a further eight western European countries overtook the UK. Since 1979, when the UK ranked 13th — see Table 5 — the UK has not regained its lead over any of these European neighbours and has been overtaken by three Asian countries plus Italy.

Table 1 reflects the triumph of the United States in the first half of the twentieth century and the remarkable rise of East Asian countries in the second half of the century. Rapid growth in Europe between 1950 and 1973 is also a strong feature of the table. It should also be noted that, in the recent past, income levels in many western European countries are fairly similar, particularly bearing in mind imperfections of measurement; for example, in 1994 the UK in 17th position was only 5.6 per cent below Austria in 11th place.

Table 2 compares living standards on the basis of the United Nations' Human Development Index (HDI) rather than GDP per person. HDI was introduced in response to concerns of the capabilities school that GDP was a rather poor measure of well-being. The exact formulation of HDI has varied somewhat, although the underlying principles have stayed the same. These estimates and the discussion are based on the 1994 version.

HDI is a composite of three basic components: longevity, knowledge and income. Human development is seen as a process of expanding people's choices. Income is regarded as contributing to this end primarily in the escape from poverty; above a threshold level it is considered to make a sharply diminishing contribution to human development, eventually tailing off to nothing. Longevity is measured by life expectancy at birth and knowledge by a weighted average of adult literacy and mean years of schooling.

The components are combined in a single index by measuring them in terms of the percentage of the distance travelled between an assumed minimum and maximum value in each case; these are fixed as the most extreme values observed or expected over a long period with a view to facilitating comparisons over time (United Nations, 1994, p. 92). HDI is (indexed life expectancy + indexed educational attainment + indexed adjusted income)/3. In each case the indexed figure lies between 0 and 1 and a higher score is superior.

The appeal of HDI lies in its emphasis on components of well-being other than income. As its authors freely admit, there are, of course, many possible criticisms of the concept — an extended review is given in United Nations (1993). The index has a limited coverage and excludes many aspects of the quality of life which the capabilities school might think important — for example, civil and political rights (Dasgupta, 1993). HDI also embodies, in effect, a weighting scheme to which objections can be made. Nevertheless, given its widespread use, it seems reasonable to inquire whether relative economic decline is equally clear on this broader measure.

The estimates reported in Table 2, which are undeniably crude and constrained by data limitations for 1870 and 1913, provide an answer to this question. The picture is in fact broadly similar but the decline in ranking not quite so great — from 2nd in 1870 to 10th in 1992, albeit not much ahead of the 16th country. Again, this relative decline comes against a background of rapid overall improvement in HDI; the UK figure of 0.919 compares with only 0.493 in 1870 which is below what the UN now considers to be a medium level of human development.

In Table 2, the relative advance of East Asia is not quite so dramatic. The rankings of Hong Kong and Singapore are held back in particular by relatively low years of schooling, an attribute on which the UK still scores quite well — 3rd in 1973, 6th in 1992. This is probably a bit misleading in that it largely reflects past rather than current levels of educational investments and quality of schooling is not taken into account other than through basic literacy attainments.

Table 3. Real GDP/Hour Worked, 1870-1992

	1870			1913			1950			1973			1992	
1.	Australia	3.32	1.	Australia	5.28	1.	USA	12.66	1.	USA	23.45	1.	France	29.62
2.	UK	2.61	2.	USA	5.12	2.	Canada	9.78	2.	Canada	19.09	2.	USA	29.10
3.	Netherlands	2.33	3.	UK	4.40	3.	Switzerland	8.75	3.	Netherlands	19.02	3.	Netherlands	28.80
4.	USA	2.26	4.	Canada	4.21	4.	Australia	8.68	4.	Switzerland	18.28	4.	Belgium	28.55
5.	Belgium	2.12	5.	Netherlands	4.01	5.	UK	7.86	5.	Sweden	18.02	5.	Germany	27.55
6.	Switzerland	1.75	6.	Belgium	3.60	6.	Sweden	7.08	6.	France	17.77	6.	Norway	25.61
7.	Canada	1.61	7.	Germany	3.50	7.	Netherlands	6.50	7.	Australia	16.87	7.	Switzerland	25.37
8.	Germany	1.58	8.	Denmark	3.40	8.	Belgium	6.06	8.	Germany	16.64	8.	Canada	25.32
9.	Denmark	1.51	9.	Switzerland	3.25	9.	Denmark	5.85	9.	Belgium	16.53	9.	Italy	24.59
10.	Austria	1.39	10.	Austria	2.93	10.	France	5.65	10.	Denmark	15.94	10.	Austria	24.21
11.	France	1.36	11.	France	2.85	11.	Norway	5.41	11.	UK	15.92	11.	UK	23.98
12.	Sweden	1.22	12.	Sweden	2.58	12.	Germany	4.37	12.	Italy	15.58	12.	Sweden	23.11
13.	Norway	1.09	13.	Norway	2.19	13.	Italy	4.28	13.	Austria	15.27	13.	Australia	22.56
14.	Italy	1.03	14.	Italy	2.09	14.	Austria	4.07	14.	Norway	14.05	14.	Denmark	21.81
15.	Finland	0.84	15.	Finland	1.81	15.	Finland	4.00	15.	Finland	13.42	15.	Ireland	20.76
16.	Japan	0.46	16.	Japan	1.03	16.	Ireland	3.80	16.	Japan	11.15	16.	Finland	20.45
						17.	Singapore	2.79	17.	Spain	10.86	17.	Spain	20.22
						18.	Spain	2.60	18.	Greece	10.77	18.	Japan	20.02
						19.	Greece	2.58	19.	Ireland	10.06	19.	Greece	16.84
						20.	Portugal	2.58	20.	Portugal	9.86	20.	Hong Kong	16.49
						21.	Hong Kong	2.30	21.	Singapore	6.45	21.	Singapore	14.43
						22.	Japan	2.03	22.	Hong Kong	5.95	22.	Portugal	14.06
						23.	South Korea	1.28	23.	Taiwan	4.13	23.	Taiwan	11.06
						24.	Taiwan	1.17	24.	South Korea	3.22	24.	South Korea	8.48

Sources: derived from Maddison (1995) and for Hong Kong and Singapore from ILO, *Yearbook of Labour Statistics* (various issues).

Table 4. Real GDP/Hour Worked, 1870-1992 (Actual & Adjusted)

1870-1913	Act.	Adj.
1. Australia	0.9	1.1
2. UK	1.0	1.2
3. Netherlands	0.9	1.3
4. USA	1.8	1.9
5. Belgium	1.0	1.2
6. Switzerland	1.5	1.8
7. Canada	2.2	2.3
8. Germany	1.6	1.8
9. Denmark	1.6	1.9
10. Austria	1.5	1.8
11. France	1.5	1.7
12. Sweden	1.5	1.8
13. Norway	1.3	1.6
14. Italy	1.3	1.7
15. Finland	1.4	1.8
16. Japan	1.4	1.9

1913-1950	Act.	Adj.
1. Australia	0.7	1.5
2. USA	1.6	2.5
3. UK	0.8	1.6
4. Canada	1.4	2.3
5. Netherlands	1.1	1.3
6. Belgium	0.7	1.4
7. Germany	0.3	0.7
8. Denmark	1.6	1.7
9. Switzerland	2.1	2.7
10. Austria	0.2	0.9
11. France	1.1	1.9
12. Sweden	2.1	2.8
13. Norway	2.1	2.5
14. Italy	0.8	2.0
15. Finland	1.9	2.3
16. Japan	0.9	1.8

1950-1973	Act.	Adj.
1. USA	2.4	2.7
2. Canada	2.9	3.0
3. Switzerland	3.1	3.3
4. Australia	2.4	2.6
5. UK	2.5	3.1
6. Sweden	3.1	4.1
7. Netherlands	3.4	4.8
8. Belgium	3.5	4.5
9. Denmark	3.1	4.1
10. France	4.0	5.0
11. Norway	3.2	4.2
12. Germany	5.0	6.0
13. Italy	5.0	5.8
14. Austria	4.9	5.9
15. Finland	4.3	5.2
16. Japan	4.3	4.3
17. Singapore	4.3	3.7
18. Spain	5.8	6.4
19. Greece	6.2	6.4
20. Portugal	5.7	6.0
21. Hong Kong	5.5	4.2
22. Japan	8.0	7.7
23. South Korea	5.2	4.1
24. Taiwan	6.2	5.6

1973-1992	Act.	Adj.
1. USA	1.4	1.1
2. Canada	1.5	1.5
3. Netherlands	1.4	2.2
4. Switzerland	0.8	1.7
5. Sweden	1.2	1.3
6. France	1.7	2.7
7. Australia	1.4	1.5
8. Germany	2.1	2.7
9. Belgium	1.9	2.9
10. Denmark	1.6	1.7
11. UK	1.4	2.2
12. Italy	2.4	2.4
13. Austria	2.2	2.5
14. Norway	2.9	3.2
15. Finland	1.6	2.2
16. Japan	3.0	3.1
17. Spain	1.9	3.3
18. Ireland	3.3	3.3
19. Greece	1.5	2.4
20. Portugal	2.1	1.9
21. Singapore	5.9	4.3
22. Hong Kong	5.4	5.5
23. Taiwan	6.2	5.3
24. South Korea	6.9	5.2

Sources: derived from sources underlying Tables 1 and 3 using method of Beckerman (1980) as explained in the text.

In the introduction it was noted that, in considering relative levels of economic welfare, it was important to look at how much work effort is required to produce GDP as well as the size of GDP per person. This is, in fact, much more important in international comparisons than is generally realised. Hours worked have changed enormously over time but experience has diverged especially with regard to Europe and Asia both as a result of changes in labour force participation rates and the length of the work year.

Given this history, although estimates of hours worked are undoubtedly less reliable than those for GDP, particularly for the period up to 1950, it is important to try and take some account of these trends. For example, the estimates in Maddison (1995, p. 248) show annual hours worked per person employed in the UK as 2984 in 1870 falling to 1958 by 1950 and 1491 by 1992 whereas in South Korea an average work year of 2200 hours in 1950 rose to 2800 by 1992.

There are some interesting modifications to the picture of Table 1 in Table 3. The overall growth of hourly labour productivity in the UK since 1870 is a good deal higher than that of GDP per person; the level in 1992 was 9.2 times that of 1870. Relative economic decline is still apparent but the UK falls less far down the rankings — from 2nd in 1870 to 11th in 1973 and also in 1992 — and remains above all the East Asian countries including Japan, Hong Kong and Singapore in 1992.

It is quite noticeable that, relative either to Asia or the USA, Europe looks much better in terms of output per hour worked than output per person. This reflects differences in age structure of the populations, retirement and holiday practices and, of course, unemployment. This should surely be borne in mind by those who compute 'competitiveness' league tables, although the implications for socio-economic welfare are not entirely straightforward and deserve some research.

Table 4 considers the period since 1870 in terms of growth rates rather than levels of real GDP per person. The periodisation is that favoured by Maddison (1995) who analyses historical experience in terms of phases of economic growth. These are punctuated by wars with 1913-50 comprising a period both of war and of the dislocation of the interwar depression. The 1950-73 period is one of generally very rapid growth followed by slowdown since the early 1970s accompanied by a renewal of macroeconomic shocks and the exhaustion of rapid catch-up growth in Europe and Japan.

The UK shares in this general experience, with 1950-73 showing the highest sustained growth rate in our economic history, but in every period it has had a below average growth rate. In 1870-1913 the UK ranks 14th of 16, in 1913-50 11th of 16, in 1950-73 22nd of 24 and in 1973-92 19th of 24. In the post-war years it is noticeable that the gap between the British growth rate and that of the fastest growing economies in the table has been much larger than before.

In Table 4 the countries are listed in the rank order of their output per hour at the start of the period. Since World War II, but not before, there is a tendency — pronounced in 1950-73 for growth rates to be inversely related to initial productivity levels as might be predicted if catch-up was a strong part of growth performance. In this regard, it is noticeable that growth of output per person in the UK appears both before and after 1973 to have been unimpressive relative to countries with similar or slightly higher initial levels of productivity.

Table 4 reports not only actual GDP per person growth but also an adjusted figure allowing for changes in hours worked. This is an attempt to follow up the arguments of Nordhaus and Tobin (1972). Before looking at these estimates, it is necessary to issue a strong health warning that imputations for changes in leisure/non-market work, while justified in theory, are enormously sensitive to methodology in practice. The approach in Table 4 is one which tends to minimise the implications relative to the alternatives and basically follows the approach suggested by Beckerman (1980).

Thus only changes in hours worked since the beginning of the period are considered and these are valued at the average wage rate in the final year. The conservative assumption is made that there is no productivity gain in leisure/non-market work. Rising labour force participation rates and/or hours per person employed imply an imputation that lowers growth rates and vice versa.

For the UK, rankings on adjusted growth are quite similar in each period to those on the original estimates. There are, however, some quite marked changes in other countries' relative positions. In the most recent period compare Italy and Spain, the USA and Switzerland or Ireland and Japan, for example. One change that does show up for the UK is that on the adjusted measure, growth in the 1973-92 period is substantially faster than prior to 1913, although the slowdown since the pre-1973 Golden Age is still nearly as large as on the unadjusted measure.

The most important result of the imputations in Table 4 is for Asia/Europe comparisons. Since 1950 the clear tendency is for these imputations to raise European growth rates, on occasion by as much as one percentage point per year. In general, the reverse is true of the East Asian countries and the magnitude of the adjustment goes as high as 1.7 percentage points for South Korea in 1973-92.

The fast catch-up growth of East Asian countries in recent years no longer appears quite so exceptional and, indeed, the adjustment proposed for changes in hours worked reduces the growth rates of Hong Kong, South Korea, Singapore and Taiwan beneath those of Italy, Spain and West Germany in the European Golden Age. To balance this point, it should be noted that the estimates of levels of GDP/hour worked in Table 3 suggest that the rapid Asian catch-up

Table 5. Growth of Real GDP/Person, 1979-1994

	Real GDP/Person, 1979 ($ Int,1990)	Growth Rate (% per year)
1. USA	18489	1.3
2. Switzerland	17800	1.1
3. Canada	16246	0.8
4. Germany	15257	1.5
5. France	14850	1.3
6. Denmark	14731	1.8
7. Sweden	14720	0.9
8. Netherlands	14317	1.2
9. Australia	13670	1.5
10. Austria	13487	1.7
11. Belgium	13457	1.7
12. Norway	13245	2.2
13. UK	13087	1.5
14. Japan	12754	2.9
15. Italy	12588	1.8
16. New Zealand	12450	1.3
17. Finland	12089	1.4
18. Spain	9488	1.9
19. Hong Kong	9276	5.1
20. Greece	9071	0.8
21. Ireland	8161	3.0
22. Portugal	7973	2.2
23. Singapore	7618	6.2
24. Taiwan	5352	6.1
25. South Korea	4350	6.5

Sources: Maddison (1995) supplemented by World Bank (1995) and Asian Development Bank (1995).

growth may continue for a good deal longer than would be supposed on the basis of comparisons of real GDP/person.

Finally, in this initial overview, it remains to consider growth in the period since 1979 when the Conservatives took office. The period is in some ways unfortunate. 1994 is not a business cycle peak and comparisons over time are best conducted from peak year to peak year, while the British recovery from the early 1990s recession was further advanced than that of most European countries.

In Table 5, the UK ranking is higher than in any of the periods in Table 4 and the growth rate since 1979 is just below the median of 1.7 per cent. The growth rate of 1.5 per cent is lower than that of the Golden Age, similar to the average over 1913-50 but above that of the pre-World War I years.

The overall picture which has emerged from this survey is easy to summarise. On all the measures considered, relative economic decline is apparent throughout the century after 1870. On most indicators, that decline appears to have been at its most rapid in the years from the 1950s through the 1970s. Since 1979 the UK's growth and productivity performance appears to have been near average for the sample of countries considered but four more countries have overtaken the British level of GDP per person.

Chapter Two: Policy Response

In this chapter further details of long-run economic performance are discussed. Here the focus is not on economic growth *per se* but on other characteristics of British economic development associated with long run growth potential. Some of these features, relating to structural change and shares of trade and patenting, are best regarded as diagnostics which can perhaps reveal something of the strengths and weaknesses of productivity performance but are not themselves policy objectives or direct measures of economic welfare.

This chapter also examines trends in the 'proximate determinants' of growth, using the traditional tools of growth accounting pioneered by Denison (1967). This provides insight into the sources of growth and thus both into why growth rates have differed and whether such differences are likely to continue. This level of explanation deals only with the ways in which growth has been achieved; it does not deal with the more profound issues of what caused levels of investment or productivity advance nor with the reasons for management behaviour or political decisions which might influence these variables.

Table 6 relates to the much discussed topic of de-industrialisation which can be defined as a declining share of employment in industry. Table 6 shows that, traditionally, the UK was among the most industrialised (and least agricultural) countries. De-industrialisation has taken place in the·last thirty years and at a pace that is rapid relative to other countries. Nevertheless, in 1993 the UK was only just below the median share of employment in industry among the countries listed in Table 6.

A high share of employment in industry is not *per se* desirable nor should it be a policy objective. If de-industrialisation is a cause for concern, this is either because it is held to be harmful to growth or because it is believed to reflect underlying weaknesses which have adverse implications for future growth potential. I have reviewed these arguments at length elsewhere (Crafts, 1993; 1996c).

A crude summary of the conclusions of those papers would be that: reductions of employment in manufacturing have been an inherent part of addressing Britain's weak productivity performance in earlier years; at the same time, the extent of de-industrialisation may well reflect weaknesses, particularly in innovation, that have been growth-retarding; and de-industrialisation may reduce future growth of real incomes through its implications for trends in the real exchange rate.

Table 7 reports a decline in Britain's share of world export trade in manufactures from 30.9 per cent in 1913 to 7.9 per cent in 1992. The decline in world market share is shown to have been exceptionally rapid between 1950 and 1973. This is slightly misleading for two reasons: (i) in 1950 British world market share was distorted by the aftermath of the war — in 1937 it was only 20.9 per cent (Crafts, 1993, p. 20); (ii) the market shares relate only to the countries in the table and, since 1973, they have collectively lost considerable ground to newly industrialising countries.

Again, these data on world market shares are principally of interest as diagnostics. In fact, effective analysis of trade performance requires more detailed information on its correlates at the sectoral level. This suggests that exporting success prior to World War II depended on traditional staples such as textiles and was not based on hi-tech sectors that were research or high-skilled labour intensive. In other words, Britain was a very different leader in world trade than was the United States after World War II (Crafts and Thomas, 1986; Crafts, 1989).

Since the war, the pattern of comparative advantage revealed in Britain's trade has changed completely so that in recent years

Table 6. Structure of Employment, 1870-1993 (%)

	1870			1910			1950			1973			1993		
	Agr	Ind	Serv	Agr	Ind	Serv	Agr	Ind	Serv	Agr	Ind	Serv	Agr	Ind	Servs
Australia	30.0	33.0	37.0	24.8	34.5	40.7	14.6	36.5	48.9	7.3	35.1	57.6	5.3	23.7	71.0
Austria	65.0	19.2	15.8	56.7	24.3	19.0	34.0	35.4	30.6	16.2	40.6	43.2	6.9	35.0	58.1
Belgium	43.0	37.6	19.4	25.3	43.3	31.4	10.1	46.8	43.1	3.8	39.5	56.7	2.6	27.7	69.7
Canada	53.0	28.0	19.0	37.1	29.4	33.5	21.8	36.0	42.2	6.5	30.4	63.1	4.5	22.4	73.1
Denmark	51.7	n/a	n/a	41.7	24.1	34.2	25.1	33.3	41.6	9.4	33.2	57.4	5.2	26.3	68.5
Finland	65.0	16.3	18.7	69.3	10.6	20.2	46.0	27.7	26.3	16.8	33.7	49.5	8.6	27.0	64.4
France	49.2	27.8	23.0	41.0	33.1	25.9	28.3	34.9	36.8	10.9	38.5	50.6	5.1	27.7	67.2
Germany	49.5	28.7	21.8	36.8	40.9	22.3	22.2	43.0	34.8	7.1	46.6	46.3	3.5	39.8	56.7
Italy	62.0	23.0	15.0	55.4	26.6	18.0	45.4	28.6	26.0	17.8	38.1	44.1	7.5	33.0	59.5
Japan	70.1	n/a	n/a	64.2	18.0	17.8	48.3	22.6	29.1	13.4	37.2	49.4	5.9	34.3	59.8
Netherlands	37.0	29.0	34.0	28.3	32.8	38.9	13.9	40.2	45.9	6.1	35.5	58.4	3.9	24.6	71.5
Norway	53.0	20.0	27.0	39.6	25.9	34.5	29.8	33.2	37.0	11.3	33.4	55.3	5.6	23.1	71.3
Sweden	54.0	21.0	25.0	46.2	25.7	28.1	20.3	40.8	38.9	7.1	36.8	56.1	3.4	25.4	71.1
Switzerland	49.8	n/a	n/a	26.7	45.7	27.6	16.5	46.4	37.1	7.5	44.9	47.6	5.6	33.2	61.2
UK	22.7	42.3	35.0	11.8	44.1	44.1	5.1	46.5	48.4	2.9	41.7	55.4	2.2	26.2	71.6
USA	50.0	24.4	25.6	31.6	31.5	36.9	13.0	33.3	53.7	4.1	32.3	63.6	2.7	24.1	73.2

Sources: Maddison (1991), Mitchell (1992) (1993) (1995) and OECD (1995a).

Table 7. Shares of Manufactured Exports (%)

	1913	1950	1973	1979	1992
Belgium	5.1	6.4	6.7	5.9	4.9
Canada	0.6	6.3	5.0	4.2	4.7
France	12.4	9.9	9.6	10.5	10.2
Germany	27.3	7.2	22.2	20.8	19.6
Italy	3.4	3.7	6.8	8.3	8.1
Japan	2.4	3.5	12.8	13.7	16.9
Netherlands	n/a	3.0	5.1	4.8	4.5
Sweden	1.4	2.9	3.4	3.1	2.5
Switzerland	3.2	4.2	3.2	3.4	3.2
UK	30.9	25.4	9.1	9.1	7.9
USA	13.3	27.5	16.1	16.2	17.6

Sources: Maizels (1963), CSO (1992), ONS (1996); percentages are based on the countries shown in the table rather than total world exports. Figures for Germany refer to West Germany from 1950·and the latest year is 1990 rather than 1992.

relatively strong trade performance is positively correlated with research intensiveness and relatively skilled workforces (Owen, 1995). Nevertheless, econometric research has shown clearly that relatively weak innovative efforts and skill formation in Britain have had negative implications for manufactured exports (Greenhalgh, 1990; Oulton, 1996) and the continuing decline in world market share may well echo this.

Innovative activities are also reflected in Table 8, albeit imperfectly. Parallel to the decline in Britain's share of manufactured exports has been a fall in our share of patents in the United States. This was particularly rapid in the period from the late 1950s to the end of the 1970s and has slowed a little subsequently. An even more striking long run trend is, of course, the rise of Japan to dominance. In 1992, however, the UK still remained the third largest foreign patenter with success stories like pharmaceuticals.

Although Britain's share of patents in the late nineteenth century was relatively high, it should be remembered that this was in the infancy of modern research and development activities when expenditure amounted to perhaps 0.1 per cent rising to perhaps 0.3 to 0.5 per cent of GDP by the 1930s (Edgerton and Horrocks, 1994). By contrast, in the post-war period spending on R & D has been much larger, generally around 2.2 per cent of GDP since the early 1960s, but has failed in the long run to match that elsewhere or to yield an equivalent output of patentable discoveries.

While Tables 6 to 8 dealt with symptoms or side effects of the growth process, Tables 9 to 11 focus on aspects of the supply-side of the economy which are proximate determinants of economic growth. Table 9 reports on schooling which is the most widely used measure of human capital formation in comparative analyses of growth. Two points stand out here. First, in the long run, years of schooling have grown more or less at the same rate in most advanced countries. Second, as with R & D, it is striking that in the

Table 8. Patents Granted in the USA, 1883-1992. (% of all foreign patenting)

	1883	1913	1938	1950	1973	1992
Australia	1.1	2.0	1.2	1.5	0.9	1.6
Austria	2.6	4.0	2.9	0.5	1.0	0.8
Belgium	1.6	1.3	1.2	1.1	1.2	0.9
Canada	19.9	13.2	6.4	11.2	6.2	4.3
Denmark	0.6	0.7	0.7	1.4	0.7	0.8
France	14.2	8.1	9.2	15.5	9.4	6.4
Germany	18.7	34.0	38.2	0.6	24.2	15.5
Italy	0.2	1.3	1.4	0.9	3.4	2.9
Japan	0.2	0.4	1.5	0.0	22.1	43.2
Netherlands	0.2	0.5	3.4	8.1	3.0	2.0
Norway	0.3	0.7	0.5	1.0	0.4	0.4
Sweden	1.0	2.1	3.1	6.7	3.4	2.1
Switzerland	1.8	3.1	3.7	9.7	5.8	2.5
UK	34.6	23.3	22.7	36.0	12.6	7.5
Others	3.0	5.3	3.9	5.8	5.7	8.1

Sources: Pavitt and Soete (1982) and OECD (1995b).

Table 9. Average Years of Schooling of the Labour Force

	1870	1913	1950	1973	1989
Belgium			8.64	10.05	11.66
France		6.18	8.18	9.58	11.61
Germany		6.94	8.51	9.31	9.58
Italy			4.92	6.59	8.67
Japan		5.10	8.12	10.18	11.66
Korea			3.13	5.34	8.65
Netherlands		6.05	7.62	8.88	10.51
Portugal			2.29	3.97	6.65
Spain			4.95	5.39	8.30
Sweden			8.43	9.02	10.82
Taiwan			3.40	5.36	7.85
UK	4.21	7.28	9.40	10.24	11.28
USA		6.93	9.46	11.77	13.39

Sources: from Maddison (1996) except UK 1870 (Matthews et al., 1982), 1913 observations from Maddison (1991), Korea and Taiwan 1950 from Maddison (1989), Korea 1973 and 1989 interpolated from Barro and Lee (1993) and UN (1993), Taiwan 1973 and 1989 from Republic of China (1992).

modern world the UK invests far more in formal education than it did in the nineteenth century.

Despite the attention regularly given to schooling in cross-section studies of growth, it may not be the most important aspect of human capital but simply the most easily measured. Broadberry and Wagner (1996) point to a substantial lag in the proportion of top management with degree level education in Britain compared with the United States from at least the 1920s continuing into the 1980s. They also stress that since World War II apprenticeship has declined in British manufacturing compared with Germany which also developed a much larger stock of skilled workers with intermediate vocational qualifications.

By 1978-79, 24.4 per cent of the British manufacturing labour force possessed intermediate qualifications compared with 60.9 per cent in West Germany; in 1989, the proportions were 35.2 per cent and 67 per cent respectively. (O'Mahony and Wagner, 1994). The absolute numbers of skilled workers in Britain was about the same in both years but unskilled workers had declined rapidly during the de-industrialisation of the period.

Table 10 reports estimates of the share of GDP devoted to non-residential investment, i.e. to physical capital accumulation. Again it is clear that the UK now invests far more than it did in the nineteenth century. In the Golden Age the UK has the second lowest investment rate and this is also true in the most recent period, 1980-93. In both cases, however, the gap to the median country is fairly small.

While capital accumulation does promote growth, it is also true that investment responds to growth opportunities. Indeed, in general this second linkage is probably stronger than the first (Blomstrom et al., 1996). It is not particularly surprising then that the UK, with less scope for catch-up than elsewhere, was not among the countries with the highest investment rates post-war. By the same token,

Table 10. Gross Non-Residential Investment (% of GDP)

	1870-1913	1930-38	1960-73	1980-93
Australia	11.7	10.8	20.2	18.2
Austria			21.1	18.8
Belgium			16.5	14.2
Canada	13.4	10.4	16.9	14.8
Denmark			16.5	13.4
Finland			20.0	17.4
France	10.1	12.1	16.3	14.8
Germany	12.9	9.8	19.6	16.2
Ireland			16.1	15.0
Italy			16.6	14.8
Japan	13.1	13.6	26.5	24.0
Korea			16.6	25.7
Netherlands		14.0	19.8	14.8
Spain			17.9	17.2
Sweden			16.8	14.0
Taiwan			16.6	19.7
UK	6.9	6.0	14.6	13.7
USA	10.4	9.8	13.5	13.9

Sources: Bank of Korea, *Monthly Statistical Bulletin* (various issues) van de Klundert and van Schaik (1996), OECD (1995a) and Republic of China, *Statistical Yearbook* (various issues).

Table 11. Accounting for Sources of Long Run Growth (% per annum)

	1913-50					1950-73					1973-92				
	Fra	Ger	Japan	UK	USA	Fra	Ger	Japan	UK	USA	Fra	Ger	Japan	UK	USA
GDP	1.15	1.28	2.24	1.29	2.79	5.02	5.99	9.25	2.96	3.91	2.26	2.30	3.76	1.59	2.39
Total Factor Input	0.48	1.00	1.57	0.94	1.53	1.96	2.71	5.63	1.71	2.34	1.61	0.77	2.55	0.96	2.22
Non-Residential Capital	0.63	0.59	1.23	0.72	0.81	1.59	2.20	3.06	1.64	1.05	1.26	0.93	1.97	0.93	0.90
Education	0.36	0.24	0.61	0.33	0.41	0.36	0.19	0.52	0.18	0.48	0.67	0.11	0.26	0.43	0.46
Total Factor Productivity	0.67	0.28	0.67	0.35	1.26	3.06	3.28	3.62	1.25	1.57	0.65	1.53	1.21	0.63	0.17
Catch-Up Effect	0.00	0.00	0.00	0.00	0.00	0.46	0.62	0.98	0.08	0.00	0.31	0.31	0.39	0.20	0.00
Foreign Trade Effect	0.03	-0.13	0.05	0.01	0.04	0.37	0.48	0.53	0.32	0.11	0.12	0.15	0.09	0.15	0.05
Structural Effect	0.04	0.20	0.40	-0.04	0.29	0.36	0.36	1.22	0.10	0.10	0.15	0.17	0.20	-0.09	-0.17
Scale Effect	0.03	0.04	0.07	0.04	0.08	0.15	0.18	0.28	0.09	0.12	0.07	0.07	0.11	0.05	0.07
Unexplained	0.57	0.17	0.15	0.34	0.85	1.72	1.64	0.61	0.66	1.24	0.00	0.83	0.42	0.32	0.22

Source: derived from Maddison (1991) and (1996).

however, the relatively low level of investment since 1980 argues against any dramatic transformation in the UK's growth prospects.

Labour productivity growth is influenced by many variables but the main proximate influences are capital accumulation, acquisition of skills, technological progress, scale economies and improvements in the utilisation of resources. It is desirable to quantify these contributions and growth accounting techniques, which are briefly described below, offer one way to do this. It is also very important to try and distinguish between transitory and long-lasting sources of productivity growth. This requires theoretical insights as well as careful measurement.

Table 11 reports growth accounting calculations from Maddison (1991) and (1996) which are the most sophisticated available. The sources of growth are divided into two: growth of 'Total Factor Input' and growth of 'Total Factor Productivity'(TFP). The former measures the contributions of increases in the available factors of production taking account both of quantity and quality; two aspects of this (non-residential capital accumulation and the education of the labour force) are highlighted in the table while other items are not reported. Evidence on the responsiveness of output to additional factor inputs can be used to weight the relative importance of growth in labour and capital inputs. Recent research tends to confirm that weights of about 0.7 and 0.3 respectively are appropriate (Oulton and Young, 1996).

TFP growth stems from increases in output over and above those resulting from additional quantities of capital and labour from better resource allocation, better technological knowledge and more intensive use of resources. To the extent that improvements in the quality of labour and capital are under (over)-estimated, TFP growth will be over (under)-estimated. In Table 11, Maddison's attempts to identify the components of TFP growth are split into five components, the last of which, 'Unexplained', is essentially a combination of the acquisition and effective use of technological knowledge and measurement error.

Some of the sources of growth identified in Table 11 are largely once and for all rather than likely to be sustained indefinitely. This is probably true of the first three components of TFP growth. Catch-up effects come from reducing the productivity gap with the leading country and will tend to peter out in mature economies. The next two (Foreign Trade, and Structural) effects refer to improved use of resources associated with trade liberalisation and the run-down of low productivity sectors like traditional agriculture which also are inherently limited in their scope.

Perhaps less obviously, it should also be recognised that, in the absence of faster TFP growth, a higher investment rate will also have a transitory effect on growth. Given that there are diminishing returns to capital accumulation, as recent research re-confirms (Oulton and Young, 1996), in the long run, the impact of a rise in the investment rate on growth of the capital stock is offset by a rising capital to output ratio.

Even the initial impact of a 1 percentage point rise in the investment rate is fairly modest — probably about 0.2 percentage points on the growth rate on the growth accounting arithmetic. The key to sustained increases in the long-run growth rate is a higher rate of innovation, and thus TFP growth, rather than accumulating ever larger quantities of the same equipment.

Obviously, the growth accounting approach is demanding of data and is potentially vulnerable to measurement problems. Nevertheless, several important messages can be extracted from Table 11 which are probably quite robust.

♦ Very rapid growth in OECD countries has been accompanied by rapid TFP growth; the slowdown in growth since 1973 in formerly fast growing countries has come both from a lower contribution from capital accumulation and from slower TFP growth but much more from the latter.

♦ Transitory components of TFP growth were unusually high in the fast growing countries during the Golden Age and slowed down thereafter. Indeed, alternative methods of implementing growth accounting suggest that these points may be under rather than overstated by Table 11 (Crafts, 1995).

♦ During the period of rapid relative economic decline in the Golden Age, the shortfall in British growth came substantially from slower TFP growth. Some of this was attributable to less scope for rapid transitory TFP growth at the start of the period but there also may well have been a substantial failure in terms of the effective application of new technological knowledge. In any event, there is an 'unexplained' shortfall in TFP growth of around 1 per cent per year.

♦ There is nothing in the behaviour of TFP growth in the UK in the most recent period to suggest that growth potential is higher than in the Golden Age; on the contrary, the opposite seems clearly to be the case.

The big picture that has been built up in this chapter comprises the following elements. First, relative economic decline has stemmed from weak productivity performance rather simply from low investment. Second, a wide range of indicators are suggestive of a relatively weak capacity for innovation lying at the heart of relative decline. Third, the growth potential of the economy in recent decades is well above that of a hundred years ago; the UK has improved absolutely since then but others have taken better advantage of increased growth opportunities.

Chapter Three: An Evaluation of the Historical Record

This chapter offers a perspective on the quantitative findings summarised above by drawing on recent ideas from growth economics and detailed research by economic historians. This is intended to guide the choice of appropriate yardsticks by which to assess British performance. It will also serve to remind us that judgements cannot be based on the raw data alone but require to be 'normalised', i.e. to allow for different circumstances.

Discussion of the record since 1979 is left until the next chapter. In considering the previous century or so, a useful dividing line for reviewing British economic growth is World War II. The general conclusion of what follows is that any British failure was much more serious during the Golden Age after the war than earlier. These post-1950 deficiencies were, of course, partly a result of the legacy from the first half of the century which was not particularly helpful in the new post-war environment.

In earlier chapters, the notion that countries achieve relatively rapid growth in periods of catch-up has been stressed. Perhaps the classic case is Japan after 1950. This idea now needs to be put in to the context of a more general view of economic growth and the forces for convergence or divergence in the OECD countries. The following discussion draws on the more extensive remarks in Crafts (1996b) and in Mills and Crafts (1996). Two key points need to be grasped.

First, 'catch-up' is not automatic nor is it necessarily complete. Catching-up requires appropriate institutions and policies to facilitate technology transfer and to prevent vested interests from obstructing the growth process. Econometric research suggests both that the experience of leading economies is not consistent with the view that productivity levels are tending towards equalisation and that countries differ in their labour productivity by more than would be expected simply on the basis of investment in human and physical capital. In other words, there is room to succeed or to fail and differences in scope for catch-up are a conditioning rather than a determining factor in growth.

Second, it is not always possible or desirable to adopt other countries' technology and this may be a further reason for persistent divergence in income and productivity levels which does not connote failure. Countries may differ in terms of their factor endowments and cost conditions, so that techniques discovered and adopted in one location are not economically rational elsewhere. Moreover, much technological knowledge is 'tacit', that is a product of experience in the form of localised learning of 'know-how' rather than 'know-why' and thus not readily communicated or made use of in foreign parts.

Bearing these points in mind, relative economic decline prior to World War II can be examined. Broadly speaking, any shortfall in British performance at this time was relative to the United States rather than Europe. In the late nineteenth century, growth potential was generally low; TFP growth in both the UK and the USA was around 0.5 per cent per year (Abramovitz, 1993; Matthews et al., 1982). During the first half of the twentieth century the United States moved to a faster growth path based on much greater technological prowess and economic scale than hitherto; Table 11 reports TFP growth of 1.26 per cent per year for 1913-50. These developments were initially difficult for all Europeans to emulate — in large part for reasons beyond their immediate control.

American advantages stemmed from ample natural resources and a large domestic market and were complemented by unprecedented investments in R & D and college education. The technological learning which accumulated in the United States was hard to transfer and often of limited relevance in European conditions (Nelson and Wright, 1992). Large markets permitted more scale economies, encouraged the development of large corporations and greater R & D whose costs could be spread over a larger volume of sales. This was a different world from that in which Britain had been the industrial leader in 1850.

Although at one time it was fashionable to allege that slower British growth reflected 'entrepreneurial failure', notably in the late Victorian and Edwardian periods, on the whole these charges have not been sustained (Pollard, 1994). Detailed studies of the cotton and steel industries have suggested that, although British managers often did not adopt American methods, their decisions were rational in British conditions. Similarly, the relatively slow move to corporate capitalism in the UK can, at most, explain only a small part of the productivity gap between British and American manufacturing (Broadberry and Crafts, 1992).

Nevertheless, institutions and policy did play some part in the widening gap between American and British growth and productivity before World War II. When there was failure to perform adequately, the economy lacked effective mechanisms to remove inefficient firms and managers. Hostile takeovers were unknown and internal control mechanisms in large firms were weak (Hannah, 1983). The exposure of the economy to adverse world economic conditions in the interwar period encouraged protectionism and the spread of restrictive practices which further weakened market disciplines on the inefficient. Finally, the tradition of craft rather than managerial control of the shopfloor was an obstacle to the introduction of American methods in some sectors, for example, automobiles (Lewchuk, 1987).

If relative economic decline prior to World War II was largely unavoidable, this seems much less true of the 1950s through the 1970s when British income levels were overtaken by so many European countries. In this period, although the UK grew faster than at any time in its economic history, the verdict must be one of opportunities missed. The following discussion draws on the more detailed treatment in Bean and Crafts (1996).

In the post-war period, the possibilities of catch-up growth were much greater than previously but to exploit these circumstances fully it was necessary to have appropriate institutions and to make the right policy choices. Technology transfer was enhanced by the further spread of multinational companies, the growing integration of European markets, European investments in higher education and R & D, and the increased codification of technological information with the result that Europe (and Japan) could rapidly narrow the large mid-century productivity gap with the USA (Nelson and Wright, 1992).

More stable macroeconomic conditions, trade liberalisation and the repairing of the damage caused by depression and war promoted structural change and rapid recovery. At the same time, the reconstruction of European economies generally succeeded in reforming relationships between capital and labour in ways which encouraged high investment in return for wage moderation (Eichengreen, 1996). Overall, for fast growing European economies, rapid TFP growth and a much strengthened contribution to growth from capital accumulation was the outcome.

The UK clearly did develop a higher growth potential in the post-war world but did not take full advantage of the situation. Even allowing for lower scope for catch-up, European experience suggests that a growth rate of 0.75 or 1 per cent per year faster was surely possible. Policy errors and institutional failings became more costly in this new environment. These seem to have lain in the areas of misdirected interventionism, ineffective exploitation of technological change, and unreformed, ultimately deteriorating, industrial relations.

During the Golden Age there was a great deal of experimentation in economic policy-making involving efforts to enhance productivity growth as well as to reduce economic insecurity and inequality. Surprisingly, to modern eyes, supply-side policy did not focus effectively on addressing market failures in human capital formation or the diffusion of technical knowledge. Instead, the thrust of policy was to subsidise physical capital, to nationalise and/or not to privatise, to finance prestige research projects notably in aerospace and nuclear power, to promote 'national champion' firms and to maintain a highly distortionary tax system. In addition, macroeconomic considerations often took priority.

To some extent, similar policy errors were made throughout Europe but overall the damage done in Britain was relatively high, as international comparisons have often shown. Thus, Tanzi (1969) concluded that the British tax system was the least conducive to growth of any OECD country that he studied, Adams (1989) found that early entry into the European Community provided an antidote to misdirected industrial policies in France absent in Britain, Kormendi and Meguire (1985) obtained econometric results to show that unpredictable macroeconomic policies hurt growth in the UK more than in any other major European economy, the share of total investment carried out in nationalised industries was unusually high and the return on it astonishingly low (Vickers and Yarrow, 1988), while Ergas (1987) contrasted the success of Germany's technology policy in speeding up diffusion with the failure of the invention-oriented British policy.

Technological change speeded up in post-war Britain but its implications for productivity growth were frequently diluted. There were several reasons for this. Changes in the capital market unleashed by the 1960s a ferocious merger and takeover boom in which pursuit of size rather than efficiency or long term investment was for many the best survival strategy (Singh, 1975). In some sectors, it seemed clear that technology was pushing in the direction of Americanisation which required much better qualified management and an end to craft control of the shopfloor. It also turned out to be difficult in many cases to negotiate the reductions in personnel that would have permitted the full productivity improvements to be obtained (Prais, 1981).

Finally, Britain did not achieve the transformation in industrial relations that happened elsewhere in Europe and remained an outlier, the only case of powerful, long-established but decentralised trade unionism (Crouch, 1993). The British system was characterised by multiple unionism, unenforceable contracts and, increasingly, by bargaining with shop stewards, while with full employment and relatively weak competition in product markets workers' bargaining power was strong. The evidence suggests that this environment, in which workers and firms could not commit themselves to 'good behaviour', acted as a serious deterrent to investment and innovation (Bean and Crafts, 1996; Denny and Nickell, 1992).

Chapter Four: Success or Failure since 1979?

Chapter One set out some basic information on long run change in real incomes, the fundamental aspect of 'national competitiveness'. This chapter appraises the record since 1979 in the light of comparative performance both over time and relative to other countries. In doing so, it will return to the difficult issues relating to assessment noted in the Introduction.

Among the quantitative details in Tables 1-5, the following key points emerged.

♦ Between 1979 and 1994, the UK fell four places in the league table of countries in terms of levels of real GDP per person but maintained its position in real GDP per hour worked.

♦ The growth rate of real GDP per person was 2.5 per cent per year in 1950-73 but fell to 1.5 per cent per year in 1979-94. However, whereas the UK ranked 22nd of 24 countries by growth rate in 1950-73 in Table 4, it was 14th of the same 24 over 1979-94.

♦ Overtaking of the UK prior to 1979 in terms of real GDP per person by European countries was quite general; none of this relegation has been reversed, but falling behind since 1979 has been relative to Asian economies.

♦ Growth rates in Britain, France and Germany have been fairly similar since 1979 and all much lower than in Hong Kong, Singapore, South Korea and Taiwan which are now increasingly perceived as the success stories to which we are inferior.

There certainly have been radical changes in economic policy under the Conservative governments which amount to a substantial break from what went before in terms of supply-side policy. Privatisation, a greater insistence on market disciplines, big changes in taxation, industrial relations reforms have all been pursued vigorously but would have been inconceivable to earlier Conservative governments. So too would have been the heightened emphasis on efficiency relative to redistribution in fiscal policy and the acceptance of short-term macroeconomic pain as a cost of improving longer-term prospects.

Political debate over the merits of this programme of reform and its impact on economic performance is generally not really about the actual outcome as such but about what would have happened under an alternative policy framework and/or government. Relevant counterfactuals might include what would have happened had 1970s style policies continued or what a 'New Labour' government might have achieved since 1979. On the former, there seems now to be a consensus that relative economic decline would have continued at a more damaging pace. On the latter, we can only speculate.

Nevertheless, it is possible to consider whether it is plausible that growth could have been a good deal faster, whether the productivity growth of the recent past is likely to be maintained in future and how good recent growth looks when other policy objectives are taken into account.

A good place to start is with the strongest productivity growth since 1979 which has been in manufacturing. This has been the subject of much more detailed analysis than the rest of the economy. It must, of course, be remembered that it accounts for less than 25 per cent of GDP. Table 12 provides some comparative information.

British manufacturing labour productivity growth since 1979 has been almost as rapid as during 1960-73 whereas elsewhere it has slowed down. This is a contrast with the 1970s and the 1980s saw a marked reduction in the productivity gap with France and

Germany which had become embarrassingly big by the late 1970s. On average, in 1989 the productivity gap with Europe appeared to have returned roughly to its 1973 level, that with the United States to the late 1930s level but the gap with Japan has continued to widen. The revival in manufacturing productivity growth stemmed mostly from reductions in employment; output rose at only 1.2 per cent per year during 1979-89.

It appears that in the 1980s the UK performed a belated catching-up exercise characterised by job shedding and closures. This outcome was associated with stronger competitive pressures and a transformation in industrial relations (Bean and Symons, 1989; Haskel, 1991; Metcalf, 1994). These findings both confirm the diagnosis of failure during the earlier post-war period and suggest that some elements in the productivity growth revival were transitory.

Indeed, a comparative regression analysis of British and German manufacturing in 1987 suggests that by then British firms were better at cost-cutting and that higher German labour productivity levels were based on a history of higher investments in human and physical capital and R & D. (O'Mahony, 1992).

There are also reasons to suppose that long-run productivity growth prospects in manufacturing are now somewhat better. The qualifications of British management have improved, the share of value added spent on R & D rose by fifty per cent between 1975 and 1989 (Broadberry and Wagner, 1996) and the share of workers without qualifications fell from 71 per cent in 1979 to 57 per cent in 1989 (O'Mahony and Wagner, 1989). Although the volume of manufacturing investment stagnated, its effectiveness surely improved; the fraction of industrial investment carried out by nationalised industries fell from 37.6 per cent in 1981 to 5.6 per cent in 1991 while foreign direct investment was 33.5 per cent of private manufacturing investment in 1991 compared with 25.5 per cent in 1981. Finally, the econometric evidence suggests that the negative

Table 12. Labour Productivity in Manufacturing

Comparative Levels of Output/Employee in Manufacturing
(UK level in each year = 100)

	1870	1913	1938	1950	1973	1989
UK	100	100	100	100	100	100
USA	204	213	192	263	215	177
Japan	n/a	24	42	20	95	143
Sweden	n/a	102	100	118	128	121
France	n/a	79	76	84	114	115
Italy	n/a	59	49	68	96	111
Germany	100	119	107	96	119	105

Growth of Output per Hour Worked (% per year)

	1960-73	1973-79	1979-89	1989-94
UK	4.14	1.01	4.13	3.95
USA	3.28	1.41	2.34	2.47
Japan	9.59	5.15	4.58	4.18
Sweden	6.25	2.65	2.53	2.87
France	6.55	4.39	3.28	3.04
Italy	6.14	5.60	3.86	3.91
Germany	5.71	4.21	1.83	2.22

Sources: Broadberry (1996) and Oulton (1995).

Table 13. TFP Growth in the Business Sector (% per annum)

	1960-73			*1979-94*	
1.	Japan	5.4	1.	Ireland	2.6
2.	Portugal	5.4	2.	Finland	2.5
3.	Ireland	4.6	3.	Spain	1.7
4.	Italy	4.4	4.	Portugal	1.6
5.	Finland	4.0	5.	UK	1.5
6.	Belgium	3.8	6.	Denmark	1.3
7.	France	3.7	7.	France	1.3
8.	Netherlands	3.4	8.	Belgium	1.2
9.	Spain	3.2	9.	Japan	1.1
10.	Austria	3.1	10.	Netherlands	1.1
11.	Germany	2.6	11.	Sweden	1.0
12.	UK	2.6	12.	Austria	0.9
13.	Greece	2.5	13.	Italy	0.9
14.	USA	2.5	14.	Australia	0.8
15.	Denmark	2.3	15.	USA	0.5
16.	Australia	2.2	16.	Germany	0.4
17.	Switzerland	2.1	17.	Canada	-0.1
18.	Norway	2.0	18.	Norway	-0.1
19.	Sweden	2.0	19.	Switzerland	-0.2
20.	Canada	1.9	20.	Greece	-0.3

Source: OECD (1996)

effects of industrial relations on investment and innovation have disappeared (Bean and Crafts, 1996).

Table 13 reports estimates of TFP growth rates for a wide sample of countries for the business sector rather than GDP. These estimates are necessarily less sophisticated than those of Table 11 and omit the government sector of the economy. It is clear from Table 13 that there has been a very general and substantial decline of TFP growth from the historic highs of the Golden Age. The UK's TFP growth has fallen by only 1.1 compared with a median decline of 2.15 percentage points and accordingly the UK has risen from 12th to 5th in this league table.

Interestingly also, TFP growth in 1979-89 is the same as 1989-94 in the UK. This, combined with similar trends in manufacturing labour productivity in Table 12, gives some reason to hope that the average TFP growth rate since 1979 is sustainable rather than seriously distorted by a temporary blip in the 1980s. While such a TFP growth trend does not represent a miracle, given the weakness of productivity growth elsewhere, it might be enough over the medium term to end, and even slowly reverse, economic decline relative to Europe.

Could the UK have grown much faster, for example, by emulating East Asian countries? The growth accounting in Table 14 suggests both that the growth of these countries offers fewer lessons than is often supposed and that the UK could not possibly hope to emulate their growth. The following points deserve emphasis.

♦ TFP growth in Korea and Taiwan (and also in Hong Kong and Singapore, Young, 1995) has not been unusually rapid for a phase of rapid catch-up growth as a comparison with Golden Age Europe suggests.

♦ Rapid growth in East Asia has owed a lot to capital and labour force growth, neither of which can conceivably be matched by the UK. Over 1966-90 as a whole, relative to Golden Age Europe, it is capital stock growth rather than the investment rate which has been exceptional; this reflects the low initial capital to output ratios which will erode as these countries catch-up. Labour input growth has involved rising participation rates and hours worked neither of which are likely in the later stages of development.

♦ Historical experience strongly suggests (cf. Japan) that the Korean and Taiwanese growth rates shown in Table 2 will start to slow down quite soon as the strength of catch-up in TFP and capital per worker wanes.

More generally, it should be accepted that raising the long-run growth rate in the UK by much is not likely to be easy. For example, the most obvious way to raise the TFP growth rate against a background of questionable innovative performance would seem to be to raise R & D — perhaps by tax incentives. Implementing such a policy has many practical difficulties (Griffith et al., 1995) but, even if it were outstandingly successful and doubled industrial spending on R & D, the historical evidence on rates of return suggests it would raise TFP growth by about 0.4 per cent and growth of real GDP per person by perhaps 0.6 per cent per year (Crafts, 1996b).

Nevertheless, there may also be some scope for rectifying what may still be an incomplete catch-up by the UK, in particular with regard to human capital per worker. It is generally agreed that until recently education and training in Britain was weaker than in competitor countries. Since the mid-1980s, there has been much greater awareness of the need for change and many reforms have been introduced. It is, as yet, quite unclear what has been achieved and it may be that further initiatives will be required. Even so, pay-offs would most likely be fairly long-term and it would be unwise to assume that growth can be increased quickly by this route.

Table 14. Accounting for Growth in Europe and Asia

	I/Y	K/K	Growth due to capital	labour	TFPGR	Y/Y
1950-73						
France	23.8	5.3	1.6	0.3	3.1	5.0
Germany	26.9	7.3	2.2	0.5	3.3	6.0
Italy	24.6	5.2	1.6	0.2	2.5	5.0
Japan	32.6	10.2	3.1	2.5	3.6	9.2
UK	18.3	5.5	1.6	0.2	1.2	3.0
1973-92						
France	21.6	4.2	1.3	0.4	0.6	2.3
Germany	22.2	3.1	0.9	-0.1	1.5	2.3
Italy	21.9	3.2	1.0	0.6	1.2	2.8
Japan	30.3	6.6	2.0	0.6	1.2	3.8
UK	18.1	3.1	0.9	0.1	0.6	1.6
1966-90						
Hong Kong	25.0	8.0	3.0	2.0	2.3	7.3
Korea	28.4	13.7	4.1	4.5	1.7	10.3
Singapore	35.8	11.5	5.6	2.9	0.2	8.7
Taiwan	26.9	12.3	3.2	3.6	2.6	9.4

Sources: Growth accounting calculations from Maddison (1996) except for Italy from Rossi et al. (1992) and for Korea and Taiwan from Young (1995). TFP growth relates to the whole economy as in Table 11 rather than the business sector as in Table 13. Investment data are for all fixed capital formation, sources as for Table 10.

Post-war governments traditionally gave high priority to short-term macroeconomic outcomes and, in effect, gave a high weight to combating economic insecurity. In doing so, they usually sought the co-operation of the trade union movement and this certainly circumscribed supply-side policy. Since 1979, the Conservatives have seen themselves as escaping the trade union veto on policy, have downgraded the priority given to economic security and have been more willing to accept macroeconomic pain to achieve long-term goals. Has this entailed a large cost in return for any improvement in growth?

Tables 15 and 16 show average inflation and unemployment rates together with the so-called Misery Index which is simply the sum of the inflation and unemployment rates for 1955-79 and 1980-95 respectively. In both periods, the UK is above the median on all these indicators. In fact, the ranking of the UK is very similar in both periods. These tables are easy to summarise; they suggest both that going easy on reform in the first period was not enough to deliver relatively good outcomes and that the more radical approach since 1979 has been associated with a pretty average deterioration in macroeconomic performance.

Another aspect of the record since 1979 is the rapid rise in inequality of incomes which appears to have been much faster than in other OECD countries (Atkinson et al., 1995, p. 80) and which reverses the gentle trend towards greater equality of the previous thirty years. How costly this is taken to be depends heavily on value judgements on which there is, of course, no consensus.

It should be noted also that consumer expenditure may be a better measure of long-term incomes than the snapshot of income from which standard inequality measures are derived (Blundell and Preston, 1995). Expenditure inequality in Britain rose only about half as fast as income inequality during 1979 to 1992 (Goodman and Webb, 1995). The implication seems to be that the economy

Table 15. Average Rates of Inflation, Unemployment and the Misery Index, 1955-1979 (%)

	Inflation	Unemployment	Misery Index
Australia	5.9	2.8	8.7
Austria	4.6	1.7	6.3
Belgium	4.5	3.5	8.0
Canada	4.6	5.5	10.1
Denmark	6.9	3.2	10.1
Finland	7.8	2.5	10.3
France	6.7	2.5	9.2
Germany	4.0	1.8	5.8
Ireland	7.9	5.9	13.8
Italy	7.5	4.7	12.2
Japan	6.0	1.7	7.7
Netherlands	5.8	2.4	8.2
Norway	5.5	2.0	7.5
New Zealand	7.0	0.3	7.3
Spain	9.8	3.1	12.9
Sweden	6.0	1.6	7.6
Switzerland	4.2	0.5	4.7
UK	7.5	3.3	10.8
USA	4.3	5.3	9.6

Sources: from Layard et al. (1994); inflation is measured by the GDP deflator and unemployment rates are OECD standardized where available.

Table 16. Average Rates of Inflation, Unemployment and Misery Index, 1980-1995 (%)

	Inflation	Unemployment	Misery Index
Australia	6.0	8.2	14.2
Austria	3.8	4.4	8.2
Belgium	4.0	9.8	13.8
Canada	4.2	9.6	13.8
Denmark	4.7	9.7	14.4
Finland	5.7	7.8	13.5
France	5.4	9.6	15.0
Germany	3.2	6.1	9.3
Ireland	6.0	14.1	20.1
Italy	9.4	7.5	16.9
Japan	1.8	2.5	4.3
Netherlands	2.3	8.6	10.9
New Zealand	8.0	6.0	14.0
Norway	5.3	3.8	9.1
Spain	8.4	18.4	26.8
Sweden	6.8	4.1	10.5
Switzerland	3.6	2.1	5.7
UK	6.3	9.7	16.0
USA	4.3	6.9	11.2

Sources: as for Table 15, updated using OECD (1996); Western Germany prior to 1991, unified Germany from 1992 on.

experienced increased volatility of short-term income flows. Comparisons across countries, however, at present have to make use of income-based measures.

Policy has played both a direct and an indirect role in recent changes in income distribution. The shift since 1979 from direct to indirect taxation and the reduction of top marginal direct tax rates have had a big effect; Johnson and Webb (1993) estimate this accounted for about half the rise in inequality in the 1980s. Changes in earnings and employment account for most of the rest of the rise in inequality and these are in turn closely related to technological change and falling demand for unskilled workers. The inability of the UK to cope with this pressure on the labour market as well as countries like Germany, despite having a more flexible labour market, may well result from the low skills of the British labour force (Nickell and Bell, 1996) and thus indirectly from education and training policy.

As already noted, any attempt to adjust growth rates on account of changes in income distribution takes us into the realm of value judgements; but so, it might be said, does the implicit assumption in the national accounts measure of real income that a pound of income received by a poor person is weighted equally with a pound of income received by a rich person whereas most people would probably want to give it more weight in terms of welfare (Beckerman, 1980, p. 51).

The most commonly used summary statistic of income inequality is the Gini coefficient (G). In effect, this implies a rank-order (poorest to richest) weighting of incomes so as to reflect the common value judgement commended by Beckerman (Sen, 1979). This is used by Atkinson et al. (1995) to calculate the 'equivalent' level of national income taking account of the 'cost' of inequality as $(100 - G)$ per cent of national income. A natural further step is then to compute growth rates of this 'equivalent income' per person, an exercise similar to the one conducted by Beckerman (1980).

Table 17. Growth of Real GDP/Person Adjusted for Changes in Inequality of Incomes, 1973-1992 (% per year)

	Gini Co-efficient		Income Growth Inequality	
	1970s	1990s	Actual	Adjusted
Taiwan	29.3	30.5	6.2	6.1
Hong Kong	41.9	45.0	5.4	5.1
Norway	35.3	32.9	2.9	3.1
Japan	34.1	35.0	3.0	3.0
Italy	37.4	32.2	2.4	2.8
Belgium	42.0	35.8	1.9	2.5
Portugal	40.6	36.2	2.1	2.4
Germany	36.0	36.6	2.1	2.0
Canada	31.6	27.6	1.5	1.8
Australia	36.7	32.5	1.4	1.7
Finland	30.7	31.0	1.6	1.6
Netherlands	28.1	29.6	1.4	1.4
Sweden	33.1	32.3	1.2	1.3
USA	34.5	37.9	1.4	1.1
UK	24.3	32.4	1.4	0.9

Sources: growth of income inequality adjusted income based on actual income multiplied by (100-Gini) using estimates from Bruno et al. (1996) supplemented by Atkinson (1995). The data for inequality are said to be comparable over time within countries but should *not* be regarded as comparable across countries.

Table 17 reports the results of this exercise for the sample of countries where data are available. A higher value for G which lies between 0 and 100 per cent indicates greater inequality; a rise (fall) in G between the 1970s and 1990s entails a downward (upward) adjustment to the growth rate. The resulting change in the British growth rate is large and makes British performance look relatively and absolutely much less attractive — on this methodology the UK goes to the bottom of the league table. It also makes the years since 1973 look much less good than what went before since any adjustment to the 1950-73 growth rate would be upward.

It must be stressed again, however, that calculations of this kind do no more than show that, if rising inequality is regarded as costly, recent changes have been large enough potentially to impact strongly on any evaluation of the Conservatives' record in seeking to reverse relative economic decline.

In sum, relative economic decline against a European peer group is probably less likely in future and there may have been a modest increase in the long-run growth potential of the economy since 1979. In that sense, 'national competitiveness' has probably improved slightly. However, there has been no 'miracle'. In today's conditions the UK would do very well even to recapture its pre-1973 growth rate. Some might see the cost of the whole experience, paid in terms of rising inequality, as 'too high'.

Conclusions

The foregoing chapters contain a good deal of careful argument accompanied by an unrelenting array of detailed tables. For those with little time and/or inclination for statistics, who are prepared to take things on trust the following are brief and rather crude summary points of what those chapters contain.

1. The long run British experience is one of relative economic decline with economic growth below that enjoyed elsewhere. Real GDP per person in 1994 was five times the 1870 level but the UK has slipped from the second highest level in 1870 to eleventh in 1979 and seventeenth in 1994. Real GDP per hour worked in 1994 was 9.2 times the 1870 level but the UK fell from second in 1870 to eleventh in 1973 and in 1992.

2. The early post-war years were a Golden Age of economic growth in Europe. At this point, the UK grew faster than ever before or since, but less fast than other European economies. The present growth potential of the economy is, however, well above that of a century ago.

3. Comparisons of economic growth need to be normalised. It is important to recognise that growth opportunities have varied over time and that the stage of economic development matters. The importance of allowing for catching-up in assessments of growth is fundamental.

4. The most serious British failures are to be found in the 1950s through the 1970s. Before World War II, our inability to keep up with the United States was largely unavoidable and was shared by the rest of Europe. Policy errors, e.g. misdirected interventionism, and institutional failings, e.g. unfortunate industrial relations, were costly in an era of rapid European

catch-up where the environment for growth was very favourable.

5. Relative economic decline has resulted from weak productivity performance rather than simply from low investment. A relatively weak capacity for innovation and for making effective use of technological change lie at the heart of disappointing British economic growth.

6. Since 1979, growth has been similar to that of major European countries but much slower than growth in East Asia. Historical comparisons suggest that these Asian growth rates are not 'miraculous' and are based on catch-up possibilities not available to the UK, involving very rapid growth of physical and human capital and labour inputs.

7. In attempting to reverse relative economic decline, the Conservatives have pursued quite radical reforms. There was a short term productivity pay-off from shaking out inefficiency. On top of this, despite continuing worries about innovation and skills, improved industrial relations, a better quality of investment and trends in productivity growth suggest that there may have been a relative improvement sufficient to prevent further economic decline relative to Europe. A new government may find it quite difficult to raise the growth rate by very much.

8. The reforms since 1979 may have had some pay-off in terms of growth but, for those whose main concern is with the distribution of income, the overall outcome might be regarded as negative. Inequality, measured purely in terms of income, has increased more rapidly in the UK than elsewhere. However, expenditure inequality in Britain rose only by about half as much as income inequality, and it is a matter for political debate, rather than quantitative analysis, whether the resultant outcome is acceptable or not.

References

Abramovitz M (1993), 'The Search for the Sources of Growth: Areas of Ignorance, Old and New', *Journal of Economic History*, 53, 217-243.

Adams WJ (1989), *Restructuring the French Economy*, Washington, DC: Brookings Institution.

Asian Development Bank (1995), *Asian Development Outlook*, Oxford: Oxford University Press.

Atkinson AB (1995), *Incomes and the Welfare State*, Cambridge: Cambridge University Press.

Atkinson AB, Rainwater L and Smeeding TM (1995), *Income Distribution in OECD Countries*, Paris: OECD.

Barro R and Lee J-W (1993), 'International Comparisons of Educational Attainment', *Journal of Monetary Economics*, 32, 363-394.

Bean CR and Crafts NFR (1996), 'British Economic Growth since 1945: Relative Economic Decline...and Renaissance?', in NFR Crafts and G Toniolo (eds.), *Economic Growth in Europe since 1945*, Cambridge: Cambridge University Press, 131-172

Bean CR and Symons J (1989), 'Ten Years of Mrs T.', *NBER Macroeconomics Annual*, 3, 13-61.

Beckerman W (1980), 'Comparative Growth Rates of 'Measurable Economic Welfare': Some Experimental Calculations', in RCO Matthews (ed.), *Economic Growth and Resources* vol. 2, London: Macmillan, 36-59.

Blomstrom M, Lipsey RE and Zejan M (1996), 'Is Fixed Investment the Key to Economic Growth?', *Quarterly Journal of Economics*, 111, 269-276.

Blundell R and Preston I (1995), 'Income, Expenditure and the Living Standards of UK Households', *Fiscal Studies* 16(3), 40-54.

Broadberry SN (1996), 'Convergence: What the Historical Record Shows', in B van Ark and NFR. Crafts (eds.), *Quantitative Aspects of Post-war European Economic Growth*, Cambridge: Cambridge University Press, forthcoming.

Broadberry SN and Crafts NFR (1992), 'Britain's Productivity Gap in the 1930s: Some Neglected Factors', *Journal of Economic History*, 52, 531-558.

Broadberry SN and Wagner K (1996), 'Human Capital and Productivity in Manufacturing during the Twentieth Century: Britain, Germany and the United States', in B van Ark and NFR Crafts (eds.), *Quantitative Aspects of Post-war European Economic Growth*, Cambridge: Cambridge University Press, forthcoming.

Bruno M, Ravallion M and Squire L (1996), 'Equity and Growth in Developing Countries', *World Bank Policy Research Working Paper* No. 1563.

Central Statistical Office (1992), *Monthly Review of External Trade Statistics, Annual Supplement*, London: HMSO.

Crafts NFR (1989), 'Revealed Comparative Advantage in Manufacturing, 1899-1950', *Journal of European Economic History*, 18, 127-137.

Crafts NFR (1993), *Can De-Industrialisation Seriously Damage Your Wealth?*, London: Institute of Economic Affairs.

Crafts NFR (1995), 'The Golden Age of Economic Growth in Western Europe, 1950-1973', *Economic History Review*, 48, 429-447.

Crafts NFR (1996a), 'The Human Development Index: Some Historical Comparisons', *LSE Department of Economic History Discussion Paper* No. 33.

Crafts NFR (1996b), ' 'Post Neoclassical Endogenous Growth Theory': What are its Policy Implications?', *Oxford Review of Economic Policy*, 12(2), 30-47.

Crafts NFR (1996c), 'Deindustrialisation and Economic Growth', *Economic Journal*, 106, 172-183.

Crafts NFR and Thomas M (1986), 'Comparative Advantage in UK Manufacturing Trade, 1910-1935', *Economic Journal*, 96, 629-645.

Crouch C (1993), *Industrial Relations and European State Traditions*, Oxford: Clarendon Press.

Dasgupta P (1993), *An Inquiry into Well-Being and Destitution*, Oxford: Clarendon Press.

Denison EF (1967), *Why Growth Rates Differ*, Washington, DC: Brookings Institution.

Denny K and Nickell S (1992), 'Unions and Investment in British Industry', *Economic Journal*, 102, 874-887.

Department of Trade and Industry (1994), *Competitiveness: Helping Business to Win* (Cm. 2563), London: HMSO.

Edgerton DEH and Horrocks SM (1994), 'British Industrial Research and Development before 1945', *Economic History Review*, 47, 213-238.

Eichengreen B (1996), 'Institutions and Economic Growth: Europe after World War II', in NFR Crafts and G Toniolo (eds.), *Economic Growth in Europe since 1945*, Cambridge: Cambridge University Press, 38-72.

Ergas H (1987), 'Does Technology Policy Matter?', in BR Guile and H Brooks (eds.), *Technology and Global Industry*, Washington DC: National Academy Press, 191-245.

Goodman A and Webb S (1995), 'The Distribution of UK Household Expenditure, 1979-92', *Fiscal Studies*, 16(3),55-80.

Greenhalgh C (1990), 'Innovation and Trade Performance in the United Kingdom', *Economic Journal*, 100, 105-118.

Griffith R, Sandler D and van Reenen J (1995), 'Tax Incentives for R and D', *Fiscal Studies*, 16(2), 21-44.

Hannah L (1983), *The Rise of the Corporate Economy*, London: Methuen.

Haskel J (1991), 'Imperfect Competition, Work Practices and Productivity Growth', *Oxford Bulletin of Economics and Statistics*, 53, 265-279.

Johnson P and Webb S (1993), 'Explaining the Growth in UK Income Inequality: 1979-1988', *Economic Journal*, 103, 429-435.

Kormendi RC and Meguire PC (1985), 'Macroeconomic Determinants of Growth', *Journal of Monetary Economics*, 16, 141-163.

Krugman P (1994), 'Competitiveness: A Dangerous Obsession', *Foreign Affairs*, 73(2), 28-44.

Layard R, Nickell S and Jackman R. (1994), *The Unemployment Crisis*, Oxford: Oxford University Press.

Lewchuk W (1987), *American Technology and the British Vehicle Industry*, Cambridge: Cambridge University Press.

Maddison A (1989), *The World Economy in the Twentieth Century*, Paris: OECD.

Maddison A (1991), *Dynamic Forces in Capitalist Development* Oxford: Oxford University Press.

Maddison A (1995), *Monitoring the World Economy, 1820-1992*, Paris: OECD.

Maddison A (1996), 'Macroeconomic Accounts for European Countries', in B van Ark and NFR Crafts (eds.), *Quantitative Aspects of Post-war European Economic Growth*, Cambridge: Cambridge University Press, forthcoming.

Maizels A (1963), *Industrial Growth and World Trade*, Cambridge: Cambridge University Press.

Matthews RCO, Feinstein CH and Odling-Smee JC (1982), *British Economic Growth, 1856-1973*, Stanford: Stanford University Press.

Metcalf D (1994), 'Transformation of British Industrial Relations? Institutions, Conduct and Outcomes, 1980-1990', in R Barrell (ed.), *The UK Labour Market*, Cambridge Cambridge University Press, 126-157.

Mills TC and Crafts NFR (1996), 'After the Golden Age: A Long Run Perspective on Growth Rates that Speeded Up, Slowed Down and Still Differ', *University of Loughborough Department of Economics Discussion Paper No. 15*

Mitchell BR (1992), *International Historical Statistics: Europe, 1750-1988*, Basingstoke: Macmillan.

Mitchell BR (1993), *International Historical Statistics: Africa, Asia and Oceania, 1750-1988*, Basingstoke: Macmillan.

Mitchell BR (1995), *International Historical Statistics: the Americas, 1750-1988*, Basingstoke: Macmillan.

Nelson RR and Wright G (1992), 'The Rise and Fall of American Technological Leadership', *Journal of Economic Literature*, 30, 1931-1964.

Nickell S and Bell B (1996), 'Changes in the Distribution of Wages and Unemployment in OECD Countries', *American Economic Review* (Papers and Proceedings) 86, 302-308.

Nordhaus WD and Tobin J (1972), *Is Growth Obsolete?*, New York: Columbia University Press.

OECD (1995a), *Historical Statistics, 1960-1993*, Paris: OECD.

OECD (1995b), *Basic Science and Technology Statistics*, Paris: OECD.

OECD (1996), *Economic Outlook*, Paris: OECD.

Office of National Statistics (1996), *Monthly Review of External Trade Statistics*, London: HMSO.

O'Mahony M (1992), 'Productivity and Human Capital Formation in UK and German Manufacturing', *National Institute of Economic and Social Research Discussion Paper No. 28.*

O'Mahony M and Wagner K (1994), *Changing Fortunes: An Industry Study of British and German Productivity Growth over Three Decades*, London: NIESR.

Oulton N (1995), 'Supply Side Reform and UK Economic Growth: What Happened to the Miracle?', *National Institute Economic Review*, 154, 53-70.

Oulton N (1996), 'Workforce Skills and Export Competitiveness', in AL Booth and DJ Snower (eds.), *Acquiring Skills*, Cambridge: Cambridge University Press, 201-230.

Oulton N. and Young G (1996), 'How High is the Social Rate of Return to Investment?', *Oxford Review of Economic Policy* 12(2), 48-69.

Owen N (1995), 'Does Britain Have a Comparative Advantage?', *Department of Trade and Industry*, mimeo.

Pavitt K. and Soete L. (1982), 'International Differences in Economic Growth and the International Location of Innovation', in H Giersch (ed.), *Emerging Technologies*, Tubin: Mohr, 105-133.

Pollard S (1994), 'Entrepreneurship, 1870-1914', in R Floud and D McCloskey (eds.), *The Economic History of Britain Since 1700*, vol. 2, Cambridge: Cambridge University Press, 62-89.

Prais SJ (1981), *Productivity and Industrial Structure*, Cambridge: Cambridge University Press.

Republic of China (1992), *Yearbook of Statistics.*

Rossi N, Sorgato A. and Toniolo G (1992), 'Italian Historical Statistics, 1890-1990', *University of Venice Dipartimento di Scienze Economiche Working Paper No. 92-18.*

Sen AK (1979), 'The Welfare Basis of Real Income Comparisons: A Survey', *Journal of Economic Literature*, 27, 1-45.

Sen AK (1987), *The Standard of Living*, Cambridge: Cambridge University Press.

Singh A (1975), 'Takeovers, Natural Selection and the Theory of the Firm: Evidence from the Post-war UK Experience', *Economic Journal*, 85, 497-515.

Tanzi V (1969), *The Individual Income Tax and Economic Growth*, Baltimore: Johns Hopkins University Press

United Nations (1993), *Human Development Report*, New York: United Nations.

United Nations (1994), *Human Development Report*, New York: United Nations.

van de Klundert T and van Schaik A (1996), 'On the Historical Continuity of the Process of Economic Growth', in B van Ark and NFR Crafts (eds.), *Quantitative Aspects of Post-war European Economic Growth*, Cambridge: Cambridge University Press, forthcoming.

Vickers J and Yarrow G (1988), *Privatisation: An Economic Analysis*, Cambridge, Mass.: MIT Press.

World Bank (1995), *World Tables*, Baltimore: Johns Hopkins Press.

Young A (1995), 'The Tyranny of Numbers: Confronting the Statistical Realities of the East Asian Growth Experience', *Quarterly Journal of Economics*, 110, 641-680.

PAPERS IN PRINT

OCCASIONAL PAPERS